KINDRED SPIRITS
EDITION
Silver Bush, Park Corner
Kensington, R.R. #2
ce Edward Island, Canada, C0B 1M0

Y0-ARM-693

FINDING
ANNE

ON PRINCE EDWARD ISLAND

ISLAND PATHWAYS

RAGWEED
THE ISLAND PUBLISHER

© 1991, Ragweed Press

editing: Kathleen Hamilton, Sibyl Frei
colour photography: John Sylvester
cover design: Sibyl Frei
book design: Sibyl Frei, Lynn Henry
printing: Hignell Printing

Printed and bound in Canada
*With thanks to the Department of Communications for its
kind support*

Thanks to Catherine Matthews, Tim Brehaut, Jean Mosher and
Sherrie Davidson for their research assistance and to Dr. Eliz-
abeth R. Epperly, Louise Polland and the L.M. Montgomery
Heritage Sites Committee (Dr. F.W.P. Bolger, George Campbell,
Barbara MacDonald, John and Jennie Macneill) for their valuable
editorial assistance.

The royalties on sales of this book are being donated to the
Lucy Maud Montgomery children's literature award adminis-
tered by the Prince Edward Island Council for the Arts. *Anne of
Green Gables* is a trade mark of Ruth Macdonald and David Macdonald, heirs of Lucy Maud Montgomery. Quotations from *Anne
of Green Gables* and other novels by Lucy Maud Montgomery,
published with the permission of the heirs of Lucy Maud Montgomery. Quotations from *The Selected Journals of L.M. Montgomery,
Volumes I & II*, edited by Mary Rubio and Elizabeth Waterson,
reprinted by permission of Oxford University Press Canada and
the University of Guelph; quotations from *My Dear Mr. M: Letters
to G.B. MacMillan from L.M. Montgomery*, reprinted by permission
of McGraw-Hill Ryerson Limited; quotations from *The Alpine
Path: the Story of My Career*, reprinted by permission of Fitzhenry
& Whiteside Limited.

Canadian Cataloguing in Publication Data

Main entry under title:
Finding Anne on Prince Edward Island
(Island pathways, ISSN 1183-5265)
Includes bibliographical references. ISBN 0-921556-17-9
    1. Anne of Green Gables (Fictitious character)
    2. Montgomery, L.M. (Lucy Maud), 1874-1942 — Homes
and haunts — Prince Edward Island — Guide-books.
    3. Prince Edward Island — Description and travel —
1981- — Guide-books. * I. Hamilton, Kathleen, 1961- II.
Frei, Sibyl, 1957- III. Sylvester, John, 1955- IV. Series.
FC2617.4.F56 1991   917.1704'4   C91-097570-1
F1047.F56 1991

Dear PEI Visitor

As grandchildren of Lucy Maud Montgomery, we're delighted to welcome you to the island she called home, and we hope that the information, directions and descriptions in this book will help you get the most out of your stay.

As you explore Prince Edward Island, we encourage you to let your mind roam free to appreciate the natural beauty that meant so much to Maud during her formative years. We're sure you'll see many of the same things that inspired her to write about this incredible landscape.

As you travel through this guide, you'll also meet some of the wonderful people who have helped to keep our grandmother's memories and writing alive. Many of our relatives still live on the Island, and in recent visits we have spent some pleasant times with them. Perhaps you will, too.

We hope that you have lots of fun while looking for ANNE in all her favourite places amoung the red sand and emerald hills of Prince Edward Island. The Island will always be a special place for us and our families. We hope this book helps to make you feel the same way.

David Macdonald and Kate Macdonald

CONTENTS

Archival Photographs:

courtesy of Prince Edward Island Public Archives and
Records Office, pages 24, 36, 42, 46, 56, 61, 64, 67, 96;
and P.E.I. Museum and Heritage Foundation
Collection, pages 47, 58.

INTRODUCTION

On Prince Edward Island, Lucy Maud Montgomery is remembered as a woman and author of great distinction. She is admired not only for her many awards and honours, but also because her words came straight from her heart, expressing the feelings of many who consider the Island to be their home. All but one of Lucy Maud Montgomery's novels are set on Prince Edward Island, and people have travelled from all corners of the world to see for themselves the place she described with such affection.

L.M. Montgomery's most popular novel, *Anne of Green Gables*, has been a best-seller for over 80 years. And no wonder: the character of ANNE is irresistible, with her red hair, freckles, imaginative spirit and deliciously big words.

How to use this book

This guidebook is designed for all those who are looking for ANNE and her creator, L.M. Montgomery, and it features the Island locations that you will most want to visit. The chapters are arranged alphabetically by location; each describes a different community on the Island, outlining the places of importance to L.M. Montgomery, and the ANNE attractions to be found there. Entertaining quotations from *Anne of Green Gables* and the other ANNE books are sprinkled through the chapters.

Each chapter is introduced by a quotation from L.M. Montgomery. Her insightful words tell of her own experience in the place, and offer a glimpse of life on the Island during her time here. The chapters are then divided into three sections: **The Setting**;

About L.M. Montgomery; and **Attractions and Activities**.

The Setting gives simple yet complete directions on how to get where you're going; describes what the place looks like; and fills you in on some interesting background information.

About L.M. Montgomery gives you a snapshot of the famous author's life and relates how the area was important to her and her writing. We will refer to L.M. Montgomery as "Maud" because that is the name she preferred — she was never called "Lucy Maud" by her very close friends and family. Quotations from Maud's journals and letters allow the author to speak in her own words about each location.

Attractions and Activities describes the places where ANNE can be found in and around the community. For instance, Green Gables House is an attraction in the Cavendish chapter, and the Lake of Shining Waters is featured in the chapter on Park Corner. Attractions that relate to Maud, such as the one-room schoolhouses where she worked as a teacher, are described as well. We have sometimes included a few historic attractions that are not directly related to ANNE or Maud — they are pieces of Island history that are worth seeing if you have extra time.

An additional feature of this guidebook is a suggested one day tour. Starting in Cavendish at 9 am and finishing in Charlottetown at 10 pm, you can visit most of the Island's ANNE and L.M. Montgomery attractions in one full day.

We suggest that this book can be used in several ways. You may want to read the book from beginning to end, as if it were a story, and then plan to visit the places that interest you most. Another option is to follow the suggested day tour, consulting the appropriate chapters for further information as you arrive at each location. Or you can simply read up on each place as you travel around the Island. Whichever way you choose, this guidebook will help you explore the Island on your own time and at a pace that is best for you, finding ANNE in both well-known and unusual spots.

One other useful reference in your travels is the PEI *Visitors Guide*. It is packed with information on all aspects of visiting Prince Edward Island, and includes organized ANNE and Lucy Maud Montgomery tours. A French version, *Guide de l'Île*, is also available. The PEI *Visitor's Guide* is available free of charge at ferry terminals and visitor information centres across the Island.

BELMONT

"This morning was one of April's darling days — warm south wind, hazy horizon mists, general summery feeling in the air. If the ground were only a wee bit drier I would start off for a walk — although Belmont is not a good place for solitary rambles at any time. There are no leafy lanes or secluded fields here as in Cavendish or Bideford. The only place is the bay shore and that is rather damp and boggy just now for promenading. One must be content to drink in from a distance its new beauty of sparkling blue waters and violet-shrouded coasts."

Journals, Volume 1, page 185

The Setting

Belmont is on the south shore of Malpeque Bay about 27 kilometres west of Kensington. From Kensington, drive west on Route 2. Turn north (right) onto Route 12 at Miscouche and drive through to Rosehill. Then turn northwest (right) onto Route 123. Follow Route 123 into Belmont.

Belmont is today, as it was in Maud's time, a thriving and beautiful farming community. On Route 123, lush green farm fields slope gently to the waters of Malpeque Bay. The bay is in clear view as you follow the horseshoe-shaped course of the road.

Belmont's busy farms are the mainstay of its economy. You will see fields of the famous P.E.I. potatoes, and a number of dairy and beef farms with their herds of cattle.

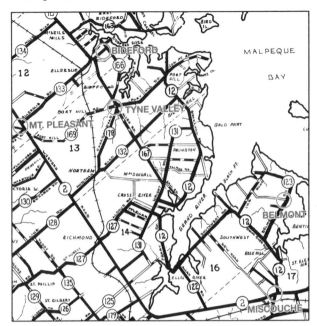

About L.M. Montgomery

Maud's second teaching assignment was at Belmont in 1896-1897. She boarded with Mr. and Mrs. Simon Fraser in a house located between the road and the water of Bentick Cove. It was about one kilometre from the school.

Maud was unhappy during her year in Belmont. She missed her close friends and found the school small and poorly furnished. "The school is situated on the bleakest hill that could be picked out. The view from it is magnificent, looking out over the head-waters of Richmond Bay. The building is very small and only fairly well furnished."[1]

The farmhouse where Maud boarded was cold. She was ill many times during that year; added to her misery was her discovery that she did not love her

Belmont Schoolhouse

fiancé, Edwin Simpson. "Was it possible I had made an awful mistake? I shiver yet at the remembrance of that terrible night. The veil seemed to be torn at once and completely from my eyes. I looked - and saw that I could not *bear* the mere touch of the man I had promised to marry!"[2] Maud broke off her engagement to Simpson not long after leaving Belmont.

Attractions and Activities

Schoolhouse/storage shed

Drive northwest about 5 kilometres past Belmont on Route 123. On the left side of the road you will see the building that was once the old Belmont schoolhouse. The old one-room school remains where it stood when Maud taught there, but is now in very poor condition, privately owned and used as a storage shed. Only very dedicated L.M. Montgomery fans, who feel they *must see* every place where Maud went, will not be disappointed.

In her journals, Maud had little good to say about her year at the school. She may have drawn on her own teaching experiences at Belmont in writing about one of ANNE'S teaching days: "When Anne arose in the dull, bitter winter morning she felt that life was flat, stale and unprofitable. She went to school in no angelic mood. Her cheek was swollen and her face ached. The schoolroom was cold and smoky, for the fire refused to burn and the children were huddled about it in shivering groups. Anne sent them to their seats with a sharper tone than she had ever used before."[3]

In the passage above, and elsewhere in her writings, Maud described the very real difficulties involved in heating the one-room schoolhouses of the time. Most often, there was only one source of heat, a little round coal-burning stove located near the centre of the room.

The Fraser House

Continue to drive further northwest from Belmont on Route 123 and you will find the Fraser House. It is about 1/4 kilometre past the old schoolhouse, on the north (right) side of the road.

This long, narrow, two-storey house is where Maud boarded while she taught in Belmont. It is a private residence and not open for tours. Maud used her journal to describe her daily routine while she lived at the Fraser house: "In the evenings, after a day of strenuous school work, I would be too tired to write. So I religiously arose an hour earlier in the mornings for that purpose. For five months I got up at six o'clock and dressed by lamplight. The fires would not yet be on, of course, and the house would be very cold. But I would put on a heavy coat, sit on my feet to keep them from freezing and with fingers so cramped that I could scarcely hold the pen, I would write my 'stunt' for the day."[4]

The Fraser House

The Simpson House

The Simpson House

The Simpson house can be found on the south (right) side of the road about 1 1/2 kilometres past the Fraser House. The large two-storey home is a private residence and is not open for tours. Ruth Lillian (Simpson) Johnson, a relative of Maud's, lives in the house today.

Maud stayed with Edwin Simpson's family when she first arrived in Belmont and often visited them during her teaching term. From the location of the Simpson house you can see out over beautiful Malpeque Bay — note Courtin Island "floating" in the Bay.

Notes:

1 Journals, Vol. 1, p. 164
2 Journals, Vol. 1, pp. 189-190
3 Anne of Avonlea, p. 95
4 The Alpine Path, p. 62

BIDEFORD

"On my way home I called into the deserted school to say good-bye to it alone. As I stood there I thought of the first day I had crossed its threshold — a trembling confused young thing feeling scarcely less childish than the children I was to govern. This has been a very happy year for me and I shall never think of that old school without a very kindly feeling."
Journals, Volume 1, page 141

The Setting

Bideford is located on the west side of Malpeque Bay. To get there, follow Route 2 west from Kensington for about 43 kilometres. You will travel through St. Eleanors, Miscouche, and Spring Hill. Just past Mount Pleasant turn northeast (right) and travel along Route 133 for about 7 kilometres, passing through Ellerslie, then continue on to the T-intersection of Route 133 into Route 12. Turn east (right) onto Route 12. Just after this turn you will cross a river. Immediately after crossing, take the first left turn onto the Bideford Road and drive less than 2 kilometres into Bideford.

Or, for a longer and more scenic drive, follow Route 2 west from Kensington for about 24 kilometres. About 5 kilometres west of Miscouche on Route 2, turn north (right) off Route 2 and onto Route 122. Follow Route 122 to the end (about 3 kilometres) and then turn west (left) onto Route 12, the Lady Slipper Drive. Stay on Route 12 for about 20 kilometres, travelling through picturesque coastal villages and Tyne Valley until you reach Route 166. Then turn north (right) onto Route 166 and drive 3 kilometres into Bideford.

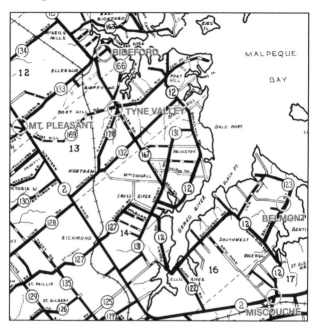

Bideford is a clean, quiet country area with a network of lovely roads bordered by the wild grasses and flowers commonly found on the Island. Some roads in the area are unpaved, and as red as those described in *Anne of Green Gables*. Stretching back from the roads is restful pastureland dotted with small woods. Bideford was once a major shipbuilding centre for the Island — since many shipbuilders were also master carpenters, examples of their huge older homes can be found throughout the area.

This is a community of mixed farming and fishing. People are also employed at the Tyne Valley Hospital, a youth centre, and local schools.

About L.M. Montgomery

The one-room schoolhouse in Bideford was the site of Maud's first teaching position, in 1894-1895. She enjoyed her year here and was fond of the school and the children. Students did not attend school regularly in those days — they often stayed at home to help with farm chores. On one school day there might be 60 students in Maud's class; on the next day, perhaps only 20 children would come.

Maud was not yet a successful author, but she continued to write during her year in Bideford. "After leaving Prince of Wales College I taught school for a year in Bideford, Prince Edward Island. I wrote a good deal and learned a good deal, but still my stuff came back, except from two periodicals the editors of which evidently thought that literature was its own reward, and quite independent of monetary considerations. I often wonder that I did not give up in utter discouragement."[1]

Maud lived at the Methodist Manse, with the Reverend and Mrs. Estey, while she taught here. In her journals she wrote of the following amusing mix-up at the Manse: "The notable incident of the liniment cake happened when I was teaching school in Bideford and boarding at the Methodist parsonage there. Its charming mistress flavoured a layer cake with anodyne liniment one day. Never shall I forget the taste of that cake and the fun we had over it, for the mistake was not discovered until tea-time. A strange minister was there to tea that night. He ate every crumb of his piece of cake. What he thought of it we never discovered. Possibly he imagined it was simply some new-fangled flavouring."[2]

Maud enjoyed the social life in Bideford. Her second cousin, Will Montgomery, lived in nearby Port Hill, and she wrote in her journals of scenic drives and happy visits with Will and other friends.

The Old School Site Monument

Attractions and Activities

The Old School Site/Picnic Area

The old school site is about 1/2 kilometre west of Bideford, on the south side of the Bideford Road. (If you drove through Ellerslie on your way to Bideford, you would have passed the old school site on your right before you reached Bideford.) The site is now a picnic area, enclosed by a wooden fence with an arched gate — it is an ideal place to bring a picnic lunch and enjoy the Island scenery. A monument marks the location of the old school building. The quiet pastureland surrounding the area is still much the same as it was in Maud's time.

The Methodist Manse

Since Maud's teaching experiences often found their way into her writing, it is likely that her first day at the Bideford school was similar to ANNE'S first teaching day at Avonlea: "The preceding teacher had trained the children to be in their places at her arrival, and when Anne entered the schoolroom she was confronted by prim rows of 'shining morning faces' and bright, inquisitive eyes. She hung up her hat and faced her pupils, hoping that she did not look as frightened and foolish as she felt and that they would not perceive how she was trembling."[3]

The Methodist Manse

The manse where Maud boarded is the first house on the west (left) on Route 166, just past the main intersection in Bideford (Route 166 and the Bideford Road). Just behind the old Manse is the modern-day United Church Manse.

The exterior of the old Manse looks very similar to the way it looked when Maud was there. It is privately owned and not open to the public, but feel free to stop your car and stretch your legs. Look for the big upstairs window on the side of the Manse facing the water — it is believed to be the window of the bedroom Maud rented.

From the old Manse you can see beautiful Bideford bay and an old lobster dock, where ships were launched when Bideford was still a shipbuilding town.

Holland College Aquaculture Centre
(The Biological Station)

Drive to the end of Route 166, about 1/2 kilometre north of the old Methodist Manse. This is the location of the biological station housing the Ellerslie Shellfish Museum. Take a few minutes to enjoy the picture displays, videos, and aquariums at the museum. You can also walk on the dock and perhaps strike up a conversation with the local fishers. They can let you know what fish are in season and tell you about the day's catch.

Green Park Provincial Park

Green Park is across Bideford Bay, about eight kilometres from Bideford itself. You can easily find Green Park by going back to Route 12 from Bideford. Turn south (left) onto Route 12. You must stay on Route 12 as it turns east by taking another left turn at the Tyne Valley intersection. Then the next left (northwest) turn will take you into Green Park.

Located here is the Yeo house, a magnificent three-storey home built by shipbuilder James Yeo. The house is open for touring, and the view from the captain's walk is particularly spectacular. Green Park has a stunning landscape — the road winds through one of the most outstanding groves of birch trees on Prince Edward Island.

While in Green Park, stop in to see the Provincial Shipbuilding Museum, which offers an exhibit on the history of Island shipbuilding, and information on how the old ships were made.

Lennox Island

To visit Lennox Island from Bideford, you must first drive back to the intersection of Routes 133 and 12 (half-way between Bideford and Ellerslie). Turn north (right) onto Route 12. After 2 kilometres, turn east (right) onto Route 163. Follow Route 163 for about 7 kilometres through East Bideford, over the causeway and directly onto Lennox Island.

Lennox Island is one of the reservations of Micmac people on Prince Edward Island. High-quality handcrafts made by people of the Micmac Nation can be found here, including woven baskets, pottery, masks, animal hides, jewellery, beadwork, moccasins, dolls, prints and paintings by First Nation Canadian artists, decoys, antique baskets and many other examples of Micmac art.

The word Micmac is an English spelling of the word "Mikmaq," meaning "the allied people."

Notes:

1   The Alpine Path, p. 60
2   The Alpine Path, pp. 74-75
3   Anne of Avonlea, p. 32

CAVENDISH

"'The Watch Tower' was the largest and highest dune of the sand-hills and the view from it is, I believe, the most beautiful and satisfying — at least to me — that I have ever beheld. I gazed at it, not only with physical eyes, seeing material beauty, but with the eyes of memory which saw all that in the past had filled it with charm for me. I could see from it almost everything in Cavendish that I ever loved — the old church hill and graveyard, the school, the woods that held Lovers Lane, the old red roads, the two ponds, the Shore Lane, my own old home site, the lovely New London harbour and New London Point, the shining sandshore, the red rock shore and the sweep of azure sea."

My Dear Mr. M., page 88

The Setting

You will find Cavendish in the central region of the Island, on the North Shore, only 39 kilometres, or a forty-five minute drive, from Charlottetown. The best way to get to Cavendish from any place on the Island is to find Route 2 and drive towards Hunter River. When you look at your map, you will see that Route 2 runs all the way from Tignish at the west end of the Island, to Souris at the east end of the Island. Hunter River is almost in the middle — 26 kilometres east of Kensington and 22 kilometres west of Charlottetown. Once you get to Hunter River, watch the signs and turn north (right) onto Route 13. Travel 16 kilometres north on Route 13. Cavendish is at the intersection of Route 13 and Route 6.

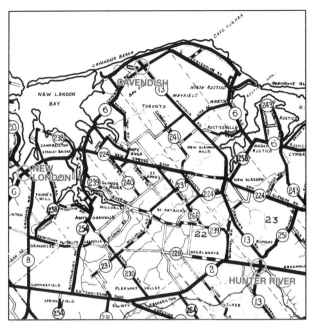

Since *Anne of Green Gables* was published in 1908, people from around the world have travelled to Cavendish to see where ANNE lived. Once you are in Cavendish, the first thing to do is park your car and step out into the fresh air. And don't worry about getting lost — this famous community is tiny. Only about one hundred and seventy-five people live in Cavendish, although hundreds of thousands of visitors come here during the summer.

In addition to being the home of Lucy Maud Montgomery and the setting for *Anne of Green Gables*, Cavendish is known for its miles of beautiful sandy beaches. Whether you like beach combing, salt water swimming, or just plain sun bathing, the beaches here are among the best in the world and they stretch on as far as the eye can see. As you walk

Cavendish Beach, circa 1895

beside the sand dunes, you may feel as though you are in a different time — perhaps treading the same path as Maud did on her frequent long walks.

Islanders and visitors alike enjoy Cavendish for the excitement of its many nearby attractions and activities. This is a favourite spot for family vacationers — there is something to keep everyone amused.

In the summer, one of your first stops in Cavendish should be the Cavendish Visitor Centre. It is located on the northwest corner of Routes 6 and 13. The entrance is on Route 13. This building houses an informative display about the Prince Edward Island National Park and other attractions around the Island. The friendly staff can answer your questions about where to stay and what to see in the Cavendish area.

Another way to discover all the attractions of Cavendish is to take a tour on a Cavendish trolley. You can get off at any stop, have a look around, and then go to the nearest Victorian-style shelter to catch the next trolley. Travelling this way instead of by car is

Cavendish Beach today

ideal for families, particularly when everyone wants to go to a different place at the same time.

Cavendish in summer means constant activity. Special events are often held, such as ice cream and strawberry socials, a variety of recreational events, and treasure hunts on the beach. Food and refreshments can be found virtually everywhere, and there are plenty of shops with Island crafts and souvenirs.

25

In recent times, tourism has become the main source of income in Cavendish, but farming is still very important to the area. For a few kilometres on both sides of Cavendish on Route 6, there is heavy tourism development. Beyond this, however, are some of the largest potato and mixed farms on Prince Edward Island.

Cavendish was named after Field Marshall Lord Frederick Cavendish in 1772. The Micmac name for Cavendish is "Penamkeak," or "sandy beach."

About L.M. Montgomery

It seems impossible to think of Maud without thinking of Cavendish. She grew up here, and even when she moved to Ontario she considered it her home. Maud's writings are lasting proof of her love for the natural beauty of Cavendish — a natural beauty that still remains.

Maud's great-great-grandfather, John Macneill, was one of the co-founders of Cavendish. Her great-grandfather, William Macneill of Cavendish, was a member of the provincial House of Assembly from 1814-1834 and Speaker of the House from 1830-1834.

When Maud was 21 months old, her mother, Clara Woolner Macneill, died of tuberculosis. Her father, Hugh John Montgomery, moved away to start a new life in Prince Albert, Saskatchewan. Maud was left to be raised in Cavendish by her maternal grandparents, Alexander and Lucy Woolner Macneill. (In fact, she was named after Lucy Woolner Macneill — along with "Maud, for myself," as she was fond of saying.)

This stroke of fate that left Maud to be raised in Cavendish made it possible for millions of people to read *Anne of Green Gables*, and to discover the beauty of Cavendish for themselves. Maud acknowledged this debt herself: "Were it not for those Cavendish years, I do not think *Anne of Green Gables* would ever have been written."[1] She also wrote: "Cavendish was 'Avonlea' to a certain extent. 'Lover's Lane' was a very beautiful lane through the woods on a neighbour's farm. It was a beloved haunt of mine from my earliest days. The 'Shore Road' has a real existence, between Cavendish and Rustico."[2]

Maud lived in Prince Edward Island for 37 years, and spent most of those years in Cavendish. Although, as an adult, Maud temporarily moved away from Cavendish to teach school in the Island communities of Bideford, Belmont, and Lower Bedeque, she immediately returned to live with her grandmother in Cavendish when her grandfather died. There she stayed for the next 13 years. During the day Maud helped her grandmother run the Cavendish Post Office, located in the kitchen of their house. In the evenings she wrote.

Following the death of her grandmother, Lucy Woolner Macneill, in March of 1911, Maud left her home and went to her Campbell relatives in Park Corner. The Cavendish home of Alexander and Lucy Woolner Macneill passed on to Maud's uncle John F. Macneill, as willed by her grandfather. Four months later, Maud married Reverend Ewan Macdonald, to whom she had secretly been engaged for five years, and moved with him to Ontario.

But Maud never really left the Island — her heart and spirit were always in Cavendish. In her letters Maud wrote of her longing for her Island home: "At times — generally in the winter twilight — I am very homesick and feel as if I would exchange all the kingdoms of the world and the glory thereof for a sunset ramble in Lover's Lane."[3]

Indeed, Maud returned to her favourite places in Cavendish as often as possible. Between 1915 and the 1930s she often travelled "back home" with her

The Site of Lucy Maud Montgomery's Cavendish Home

husband and her two sons, Chester and Stuart. These visits soothed her and gave her the energy to continue her work as a successful author, minister's wife, and mother. "Then I went up to Cavendish. Delight Again. Some old gladness always waits there for me and leaps into my heart as soon as I return. "[4] Maud's visits meant a great deal of excitement in Cavendish — friends and relatives welcomed the now-famous author home again.

When Lucy Maud Montgomery died in 1942, her body was brought home to be buried in the Cavendish cemetery. She rests now in the place she loved, never to leave again.

Attractions and Activities

The Site of Lucy Maud Montgomery's Cavendish Home

This peaceful historic site is on Route 6 (the main road in Cavendish), just east of Route 13. It is 150

Bookstore on the Site

metres east of the Green Gables Post Office, next to the Cavendish United Church.

This is where Maud Montgomery wrote *Anne of Green Gables.* "I wrote it in the evenings after my regular day's work was done, wrote most of it at the window of the little gable room which had been mine for many years."[5]

The Macneill property has been passed down from father to son for generations. John and Jennie Macneill now live on the farmland. John is a great-grandson of Alexander and Lucy Woolner Macneill (Maud's grandparents). The stone cellar of the homestead is still there, surrounded by flowers and the big old apple trees, poplars, birches, and spruces. Standing here you can see for yourself the Island countryside that Maud loved.

This was Maud's home from 1876 to 1911 — you may be able to still feel her presence as you hear the rustle of the poplar leaves and smell the clover from the nearby fields. Around the home are vegetable and flower gardens, and beds of marigolds surrounding old apple trees dating from Maud's time. The woods are alive with birch, poplar, and spruce. It is a quiet, beautiful spot.

A bookstore is located on the property, and visitors can purchase books by and about Lucy Maud Montgomery. Also kept here are the original desk, stamp and scales that Maud used at the post office in the kitchen of her grandparents' home.

Green Gables House

The turn-off to Green Gables House is off Route 6, just west of the intersection of Routes 6 and 13. It was once the farmhouse of Margaret and David Macneill, cousins of Maud's grandfather. Maud visited their farm often as a child and later based the setting of her novel *Anne of Green Gables* on the home and its surroundings.

In her novel, Maud named it Green Gables, home of MARILLA and MATTHEW CUTHBERT and, of course, ANNE SHIRLEY.

Green Gables was as dear to ANNE as Maud's own home in Cavendish was to her. ANNE was terribly homesick when she left Green Gables to study at Queen's Academy in Charlottetown: "... a horrible choke came into her throat as she thought of her own white room at Green Gables, where she would have the pleasant consciousness of a great green still outdoors, of sweet peas growing in the garden, and moonlight falling on the orchard, of the brook below the slope and the spruce boughs tossing in the night wind beyond it, of a vast starry sky, and the light from Diana's window shining out through the gap in the trees."[6]

Because of its significance to the writing of L.M. Montgomery, Green Gables House and the surrounding farmland were preserved by the Federal Government within Prince Edward Island National Park in 1937. Since then, the home has been restored and

Green Gables House

Anne's Room, Green Gables House

P.E.I. National Park
Monument

furnished as it would have been in ANNE'S day — it portrays the late 1880s period described in the novel. Outside Green Gables House, a National Historic Site monument has been erected to commemorate the literary works of L.M. Montgomery.

Prince Edward Island National Park

Prince Edward Island National Park actually stretches out over 40 kilometres of coastline, from New London Bay in the west to Tracadie Bay in the east. Maud spent many hours walking along Cavendish lanes bordered by apple trees and wild roses, then down to the dunes with their panoramic views of the ocean. As well, the National Park preserves some of the places that Maud loved and wrote about. In the park, off Route 6 just west of Route 13, you

Lover's Lane

will find Green Gables House, Lover's Lane, ANNE'S Babbling Brook and the Haunted Wood.

More than half a million people come here each summer. Many come to see the setting that inspired Maud to write *Anne of Green Gables*, but you certainly don't have to be a fan of the famous author to enjoy the park. Along with the dunes, beach and ocean, visitors here can enjoy freshwater ponds, salt marshes, red sandstone cliffs and a wide variety of birds. To see some outstanding coastal scenery, take a drive through the park. There are plenty of rest stops and picnic sites along the way.

During the summer months, a wide variety of National Park activities explain the natural and cultural features of the park to visitors. Several events focus on L.M. Montgomery and ANNE. For more information, inquire at the Cavendish Visitor Centre.

Lover's Lane

You can find signs to Lover's Lane near Green Gables House. A walk down this old farm lane should give you the same feeling of peaceful energy as it did Maud. She named it Lover's Lane when she was a child, and it was one of her favourite places. Maud passed along her habit of giving names to favourite places to ANNE: "Lover's Lane opened out below the orchard at Green Gables and stretched far up into the woods to the end of the Cuthbert farm. It was the way by which the cows were taken to the back pasture and the wood hauled home in winter. Anne had named it Lover's Lane before she had been a month at Green Gables. 'Not that lovers ever really walk there,' she explained to Marilla, 'but Diana and I are reading a perfectly magnificent book and there's a Lover's Lane in it. So we want to have one, too. And it's a very pretty name, don't you think? So romantic! We can imagine the lovers into it, you know. I like that lane because you can think out loud there without people calling you crazy.' "[7]

If you continue along Lover's Lane, you will reach the Balsam Hollow Trail, which leads through beautiful, shady woodlands alongside ANNE'S Babbling Brook. Signs along the way address Maud's love for the natural beauty of the area.

The Haunted Wood

Near Green Gables house you can find signs to the Haunted Wood Trail. The trail leads to the Cavendish cemetery, where Maud is buried. The spruce grove bordering the cemetery was the site of Maud's Cavendish schoolhouse. Unfortunately, the school itself was torn down many years ago.

As a child, Maud created her own Haunted Wood — she and her friends craved excitement in their lives, so they pretended that ghosts haunted a nearby spruce grove. When Maud wrote about it later, the Haunted Wood became the setting for some of the scenes in *Anne of Green Gables*. "A haunted wood is so very romantic, Marilla. We chose the spruce grove

The Haunted Wood

because it's so gloomy. Oh, we have imagined the most harrowing things. There's a white lady walks along the brook just about this time of night and wrings her hands and utters wailing cries. She appears when there is to be a death in the family. And the ghost of a little murdered child haunts the corner up by Idlewild; it creeps up behind you and lays its cold fingers on your hands — so. Oh, Marilla, it gives me a shudder to think of it. "[8]

If you are not afraid of ghosts, take a walk along the Haunted Wood Trail. Signs mark important features in the area and provide insight into the similarities between Maud's Cavendish and ANNE'S Avonlea.

Cavendish Cemetery, circa 1890

Grave of Clara Woolner Macneill (left); shared grave
of Lucy Maud Montgomery and Ewan Macdonald
(right)

Cavendish Cemetery

The cemetery is on the southwest corner of the intersection of Routes 6 and 13. A large memorial arch engraved "Resting Place of L.M. Montgomery" marks the entrance. Maud chose her own plot at the top of the hill, overlooking the pond, the sand dunes, the harbour, and all her most-loved places in Cavendish.

Maud shares a gravestone with her husband, Ewan Macdonald. Her plot is close to the grave of her mother, Clara Macneill Montgomery, and to the grandparents who raised her, Lucy Woolner Macneill and Alexander Macneill. Don't be afraid that you are intruding on sacred ground — Maud herself was fond of walking in the Cavendish Cemetery.

"One evening I spent wandering about the graveyard where so many of our dead people lie. It was not a sorrowful tryst. I felt very happy and among friendly presences. I felt again acutely the peculiar, indefinable charm of P.E. Island. A certain wellspring of fancy which I thought had gone dry in me bubbled up as freshly as of old."[9]

Green Gables Post Office

The Green Gables Post Office is on the southeast corner of the intersection of Routes 6 and 13, a few hundred metres from the site of Maud's Cavendish home, close to the United Church.

The building resembles the original Macneill homestead where Maud was raised by her grandparents. The Macneills were the postmasters for the Cavendish area, and the post office was located in the kitchen of their old farmhouse. When her grandfather died, Maud assisted her grandmother with the postmaster duties. Having a post office in her kitchen was a help to Maud — her stories were not always accepted by publishers, and it saved a great deal of embarrassment to have rejection letters come directly to her home. No one knew, and the writer could suffer her disappointments in secret.

An exhibit at the post office shows how Maud helped her Macneill grandparents run the post office from their home and traces the route of a manuscript Maud mailed to her publishers. The heritage postal artifacts, dramatic ice boat model and video presentation appeal to all ages.

Cavendish Church

The Cavendish United Church is beside the Green Gables Post Office on Route 6, just east of Route 13. Maud was choir director, organist and Sunday School teacher at this church, although it was Presbyterian in her day. In fact, it was through the church that Maud met her husband, Reverend Ewan Macdonald. He was the minister here from 1903-1906.

In 1974, a memorial window was placed in the church in honour of Lucy Maud Montgomery's 100th birthday. It was the Cavendish community's way of celebrating Maud's memory.

Notes:

1   The Alpine Path, p. 52
2   The Alpine Path, p. 73
3   My Dear Mr. M., p. 64
4   My Dear Mr. M., p. 115
5   The Alpine Path, p.72
6   Anne of Green Gables, p. 279
7   Anne of Green Gables, pp. 105-106
8   Anne of Green Gables, p. 164
9   My Dear Mr. M., pp. 88-89

CHARLOTTETOWN

*"When I was a child a trip to town and a trip
to Park Corner were the only outings that
ever entered my life and both were looked
upon as great pleasures. A trip to Park Corner was of comparatively common occurrence
— usually twice a year. A trip to town was a
very rare treat — once in two or three years —
and loomed up about the same proportion of
novelty, excitement and delight as a trip to
Europe would now."*

Journals, Volume 1, page 348

The Setting

To get to Charlottetown from the Wood Islands
ferry terminal, you take the first left turn after you
leave the ferry compound, and drive west on Route 1,
the Trans-Canada Highway. Stay on Route 1 all the
way to Charlottetown (61 kilometres). Just before
you get to Charlottetown, you will cross the Hillsborough Bridge. As you cross, look to your west (left)
and you will see cormorants and other shorebirds
nesting on one of their favourite places, the pilings of
the old bridge. When you exit the bridge you will be
on Grafton Street, which takes you to the heart of
Charlottetown.

If you are coming from the Borden ferry terminal,
you will find Charlottetown by driving 56 kilometres
east on Route 1. Green and gold farm fields and deep
red soil stretch back from the road as you drive
through some of the prettiest farm communities on
the Island. Stay on Route 1 and it will take you to
University Avenue, one of the main streets in Charlottetown and a direct connection with the downtown
area.

Charlottetown is the capital of Prince Edward Island and has the distinction of being the "Birthplace of Confederation". It is a clean city. The streets are decorated in summer with colourful flower baskets, and lined with lovely old trees. Alongside the modern city buildings, you will find many graceful old mansions and sites of historic importance, tastefully cared for.

For Islanders, going to "town" means getting dressed up, seeing the sights and meeting old friends on the street corner. The excitement of going to town has been a part of Island life for years: "Their sojourn in town was something that Anne and Diana dated from for years. From first to last it was crowded with delights."[1]

Many provincial government offices are located in Charlottetown. In fact, the provincial government is the largest employer here. Also located in Charlottetown are several federal government offices, including headquarters of the federal Department of Veterans Affairs.

The city has a thriving business community — people from all over the Island come here to shop and do business, and tourism is a major part of Charlottetown's economy. As well, the University of Prince Edward Island, The Atlantic Veterinary College, Holland College, the Atlantic Police Academy and the Culinary Institute of Canada bring new people to the area each year.

Charlottetown was named by surveyor Samuel Holland in 1765, for Queen Charlotte, wife of King George III of England.

About L.M. Montgomery

Maud's earliest memories of Charlottetown date from when she was about five or six years old. In her journals she describes her fascination with the city and her delight at looking in the shop windows. "Grandfather, grandmother, father and I all went to town in a big double seated wagon. To go anywhere with father was sheer happiness for me. I had a glorious day of it but the most delightful part was a tiny adventure I had just before leaving for home. The others had met some friends at a street corner and stopped to talk. Finding that I wasn't being 'looked after' I promptly shot down a nearby street in search of adventures. It was *so* jolly and independent to be walking down a street alone!"[2]

To earn her teaching license, Maud studied at Charlottetown's Prince of Wales College on Kent Street from 1893-94. In her journals Maud wrote, "I love going to college. It is simply delightful."[3]

Downtown Charlottetown, circa 1894

When her college term began in September, 1893, Maud boarded with Mrs. Alexander MacMillan on Hillsborough Street very near the college. Then in October Mrs. MacMillan moved with her family and her boarders to a double tenement on Fitzroy Street, and Maud moved with them. She lived at the Fitzroy Street house, a longer walk from the college, for the remainder of the year.

Maud's description of Queen's Academy in *Anne of Green Gables* was based on her experiences at Prince of Wales College. In 1969, and act of the Prince Edward Island Legislature amalgamated Prince of Wales College with St. Dunstan's University, to form the present-day University of Prince Edward Island (UPEI). UPEI is located on the former St. Dunstan's campus, on University Avenue.

The former Prince of Wales College is now the main building of Prince Edward Island's technical institute, Holland College. The college's Montgomery Hall on Kent Street, originally built to house women residents, was named in honour of L.M. Mont-

The Confederation Centre of the Arts

gomery. It now houses the Culinary Institute of Canada. Its dining room, the Lucy Maud Room, was also named for the famous author.

Attractions and Activities

Confederation Centre of the Arts

The Confederation Centre is a modern building located in the heart of downtown Charlottetown, on the southeast corner of Queen and Grafton Streets. The Centre, as it is commonly called, was built in 1964 to celebrate the 100th anniversary of the historic meeting of the Fathers of Confederation.

The Centre is open year-round, with longer hours during July and August, when visitors are welcome to take free tours without advanced booking. The Centre has two theatres, two art galleries, the Provincial Library, display areas and a restaurant. Many of L.M. Montgomery's original manuscripts, personal scrapbooks and other belongings are in the collection of the Confederation Centre Art Gallery and Museum. Occasionally, some of these items are displayed in the gallery.

The Centre's main theatre hosts the annual Charlottetown Festival musical production, Anne of Green Gables. The famous show plays to packed audiences all summer long. Dedicated players, musicians and stagehands bring ANNE alive before your eyes! You can see a matinee or an evening performance, but you should be sure to pick up your tickets ahead of time, to avoid being disappointed.

Province House National Historic Site

Province House is an historic building located on Richmond Street, just east of Queen Street and next to the Confederation Centre of the Arts. It was designed by Isaac Smith, a local architect, and built and furnished by local craftspeople using local material except for the Nova Scotia sandstone of the exterior walls. It opened in 1847.

Province House is known as the "Birthplace of Canada". In 1864, the Fathers of Confederation met in the Council Chamber of Province House for the Conference on Confederation which led to the formation of the Dominion of Canada in 1867. Maud's grandfather, Senator Donald Montgomery of Park Corner, was a familiar face at Province House.

To this day, the provincial legislature meets in the Legislative Chamber. Many of the offices have been restored and are used as federal and provincial government offices. The building is open to the public, and visitors can take a tour, watch an audio-visual presentation on Confederation and view displays and artifacts of historic significance.

Ardgowan National Historic Site

Ardgowan is located on Mt. Edward Road in Charlottetown, at the intersection of Mt. Edward Road and Palmers Lane, on the southeast corner. The house and grounds form a national historic site, commemorating one of the the Island Fathers of Confederation, William Henry Pope.

In the mid-nineteenth century, Ardgowan was the Pope family home. He was a lawyer, the controversial editor of a Charlottetown newspaper and a prominent Conservative politician. Pope was strongly in favour of Confederation — he participated in the Conference on Confederation and advocated Confederation for Prince Edward Island in the legislature and through his newspaper. When PEI rejected Confederation in 1866, Pope resigned from the government. In 1873, however, PEI finally joined Confederation and Pope was appointed judge of the Prince County court.

The federal government acquired Ardgowan in 1967 and carefully restored the grounds to illustrate the garden fashions of Pope's time. An interpretive exhibit has been installed to give visitors a sense of Island life in the Confederation era. The district office of the Canadian Parks Service is now located in the house.

Harness Racing

You will find the Charlottetown Driving Park at the northeast end of the city on Kensington Road. The Charlottetown Driving Park opened with its first harness race in 1890. Today, harness racing occurs three days a week and twice daily during Old Home Week in August. Racing schedules are available at the driving park.

As the horses thunder to the finish line you may experience emotions akin to those felt by ANNE, when she attended horse races in Charlottetown: "I don't think, though, that I ought to go very often to horse races, because they *are* awfully fascinating. Diana got so excited that she offered to bet me ten cents that the red horse would win. I didn't...because I

Harness Racing at the Charlottetown Driving Park, circa 1895

wanted to tell Mrs. Allan all about everything, and I felt sure it wouldn't do to tell her that. It's always wrong to do anything you can't tell the minister's wife."[4]

Old Home Week

The entire city of Charlottetown seems to go on holiday for the annual mid-August Provincial Exhibition and celebration of Old Home Week. The festivities are held on the grounds of the Charlottetown Civic Centre on Kensington Road, just beside the Charlottetown Driving Park.

The week has many special events, the most popular of which are the Gold Cup and Saucer race, and the colourful Gold Cup parade at the end of the week. Charlottetown residents crowd the streets of the downtown area to watch the parade. Maud must have drawn upon her own childhood experiences of Charlottetown during the Provincial Exhibition, when she wrote about ANNE'S amazement at the crowds in town: "There were thousands of people

The old Charlottetown Train Station, circa 1908

there, Marilla. It made me feel dreadfully insignificant."[5]

The variety of livestock at the Provincial Exhibition still brings in large crowds. People come from all over the Island and from the mainland to enjoy ferris wheel rides, carnival games and harness racing. Displayed at the Provincial Exhibition are some of the best Island-made quilts, as well as other crafts. Like ANNE, you may get caught up in the excitement: "I don't really know which department was the most interesting. I think I liked the horses and the flowers and the fancy work best."[6]

Notes:

1   Anne of Green Gables, p. 233
2   Journals, Vol. 1, p. 348
3   Journals, Vol. 1, p. 93
4   Anne of Green Gables, p. 234
5   Anne of Green Gables, p. 234
6   Anne of Green Gables, p. 233

FRENCH RIVER

"Away to the westward, across the harbor, the view was bounded by New London Cape, a long sharp point running far out to sea. In my childhood I never wearied of speculating on what might be beyond that point — a very realm of enchantment I felt sure. Even when I gradually grew into the understanding that beyond it was merely another reach of shore just like our own it still held a mystery and a fascination for me. I longed to stand out on that remote purple peak, beyond which was the land of lost sunsets. Of late years a new charm has been added to it — a revolving light which, seen from here, flashes on the point in the dusk of summer nights like a beacon 'on the foam of perilous seas in fairylands forlorn.'"

My Dear Mr. M., page 45

The Setting

From Kensington, take Route 6 and drive east for 11 kilometres through Margate and Clinton to New London. Or from Cavendish, take Route 6 west for 11 kilometres through Bayview and Stanley Bridge to New London. In New London, turn north onto Route 20 and follow it about 7 kilometres into French River.

This tiny fishing village nestles alongside the French River inlet that opens out into New London Bay. Behind the village the land slopes up through gentle hills to the rugged sandstone cliffs of Cape Tryon. Up here you can feel the full force of the northwest gales that batter the shore. But in the sheltered cove below, the fishing boats are anchored safely against the village wharves.

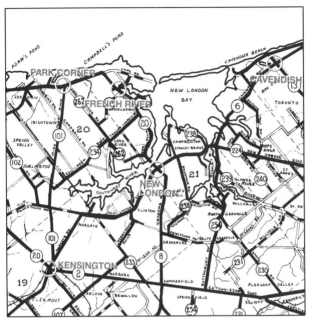

The boats are taken out into the harbour each morning to haul in the day's catch from the lobster traps. In recent years the cultured mussel fishery has grown dramatically, and there is a busy mussel processing plant just a few miles away in Springbrook. As well, several large potato farms provide rich harvest from the land that surrounds the inlet.

The first known mention of the name French River dates back to 1775. Benjamin Chappell, an immigrant living in New London, referred to the French River in his diary.[1] It is likely that English immigrants coined the name because of the Acadian French who were already living there when they arrived.

49

French River

About L.M. Montgomery

Maud spent many of her summer days on the Cavendish Shore. From there she could look across the Bay to New London Cape — now known as Cape Tryon. Maud was right about the "realm of enchantment" that lay just beyond the Cape — and she was to re-create it in her book, *Anne's House of Dreams*. The main setting of that story, Four Winds Harbour, is modelled on New London Harbour.[2]

When Maud was a child, older folks often told stories about the Maritime coast. Her grandfather "liked a dramatic story, had a good memory for its fine points and could tell it well."[3] When Maud wrote *Anne's House of Dreams*, she used some of his stories and put them in the mouth of CAPTAIN JIM, the lighthouse keeper on Four Winds Point.

The lighthouse that Maud refers to in the opening quotation is the one on Cape Tryon. In her day, its revolving white light was operated manually by the keeper to warn ships away from dangerous rocks. A second lighthouse at the New London harbor entrance gave off a steady red light, which guided ships safely into the harbor. There is still a flashing light on Cape Tryon but it's not the same one that Maud saw. In the early 1960s the old lighthouse was moved and is now a cottage on Cousin's Shore. The new lighthouse is electrically operated.

Attractions and Activities

Anne's House of Dreams

From the village centre in French River, follow Route 263 northeast for less than 2 kilometres to the Cape Road. Anne's House of Dreams is on the left just before the Cape Road.

The owner, Wilbur Lamont, has tried to depict the house that ANNE and GILBERT lived in as newlyweds. This particular house, however, is not the real-life inspiration behind Maud's description of ANNE'S house — only people who want to see everything having to do with ANNE won't be disappointed.

The latest addition to the grounds is a reconstruction of the Avonlea Schoolhouse, restored inside to resemble the school house in Cavendish that originally inspired Maud. In *Anne of Green Gables*, ANNE and GILBERT first meet at the school. It wasn't a case of love at first sight, however. GILBERT wasn't used to girls ignoring him, and to attract ANNE'S attention, he made the mistake of poking fun at her red hair. "Then Anne looked at him with a vengeance! She did more than look. She sprang to her feet, her bright fancies fallen into cureless ruin. She flashed one indignant glance at Gilbert from eyes whose angry sparkle was swiftly quenched in equally angry tears. 'You mean, hateful boy!' she exclaimed passionately. 'How dare you!' And then — Thwack! Anne had brought her slate down on Gilbert's head and cracked it—slate, not head—clear across."[4]

The "Avonlea" Schoolhouse

Lighthouse on Cape Tryon

From French River, follow Route 263 northeast for less than 2 kilometres to the Cape Road (Anne's House of Dreams is on the left just before the Cape Road). Turn west (left) and follow the Cape Road for another kilometre. The Lighthouse on Cape Tryon can be reached by following the small lane to the north (right).

In *Anne's House of Dreams*, ANNE and GILBERT spent many an autumn evening at the lighthouse listening to CAPTAIN JIM'S stories. "He told how his vessel had been run down by a steamer; how he had been boarded by Malay pirates; how his ship had caught fire; how he helped a political prisoner escape from a South African republic; how he had been wrecked one fall on the Magdalens and stranded there for the winter; how a tiger had broken loose on board ship; how his crew had mutinied and marooned him on a barren island—these and many other tales, tragic or humorous or grotesque, did Captain Jim relate."[5]

Birdwatchers will be delighted to see the cormorants nesting on the cliffs below the Cape. It is believed to be the only place in North America where the Great Cormorant and the Double-crested Cormorant nest together. Please be careful, though, not to disturb the nests.

Notes:

1   French River and Park Corner History, P. 11
2   Journals, Vol. 2, p. 222
3   Journals, Vol. 1, p. 352
4   Anne of Green Gables, pp. 111-112
5   Anne's House of Dreams, pp. 144-145

HUNTER RIVER

"This morning I had to rise with the lark to catch the early train. The ride out to Hunter River was charming. The country is a veritable 'garden of Eden' now, with all the blossoms out."

Journals, Volume 1, page 137

The Setting

When you look at your map of PEI, you will see that Route 2 runs all the way from Tignish at the west end of the Island to Souris at the east end. You will find Hunter River on Route 2, almost in the middle of the Island, about 26 kilometres east of Kensington and 22 kilometres west of Charlottetown.

If you arrive on the Island from the ferry at Borden, follow the traffic out of the village. About 8 kilometres out of Borden, you will come to an underpass. Follow the signs for Charlottetown and you'll be heading east on Highway 1, the Trans-Canada. After driving for about 11 kilometres you'll come to the village of Crapaud. When you get to the bottom of the steep curving hill into the village, turn northeast (left) onto Route 13. Hunter River is about 21 kilometres further on Route 13. You'll pass through Kelly's Cross and Brookvale on your way.

People often fall in love with Hunter River the moment they come over the top of the hill into town and see spread before them an Island feast for the eyes. The river cuts through wooded hills that surround the village on all sides. Here and there, fields of grain ripples in the breeze. Cattle graze quietly on hillside pastures, and in the valley that marks the village centre, a pond sparkles in the sunshine.

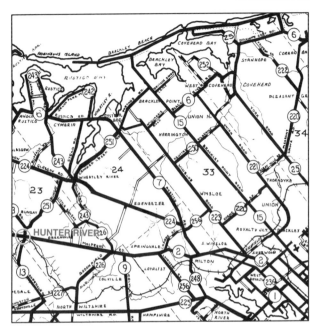

Much of the Hunter River area is prime farm land, supporting a thriving dairy industry. Grain and hay are grown for winter feed. Herds of Holstein and Ayreshire cattle provide whole milk to the local dairy. Not all of the hay goes to the cows, however — Hunter River farmers have a distinguished history in Island harness racing. Although there's no local track, horses are often trucked to the races in nearby Charlottetown and Summerside.

There are conflicting opinions over the origin of the name Hunter River. It is probably named after Thomas Orby Hunter, who was Lord of the British Admiralty in the mid-eighteenth century.

Hunter River, circa 1915

About L.M. Montgomery

In Lucy Maud Montgomery's time Hunter River was a thriving community, largely because of the railroad, which provided farmers in the area with a way to send their produce to market. The steady flow of rail passengers through the village supported many local businesses. For Maud, Hunter River was where she went to take the train to "town", saving her the long, tiring trip by horse and buggy.

In her journals Maud tells the amusing story of her trip to Hunter River to meet Earl Grey, the Governor General of Canada, in 1910. He had asked to meet the famous Island author. Maud referred to the invitation as "something of an honor—but rather an unwelcome one."[1] Having nothing suitable to wear, she had to make arrangements for a dress to be made; then she had to go to Charlottetown to select material. "I started for the station at eight o'clock, rattling along in Pierce Macneill's old wagon which is decidedly the worse for wear and giggling to myself over what Earl Grey and his staff would think if they could see my equipage and steed! I arrived at Hunter River just in time to escape the rain which began to come down heavily as the train started."[2]

Maud was soon to lose her fear of making a good impression on the Governor General. They met, and went for a walk together. Earl Grey led the way to a small white building and sat down on the steps to have a chat with Maud. However, he wasn't very familiar with country living and didn't realise he was sitting on the steps of the outhouse. Maud had a hard time containing her laughter. "I was mortally afraid that some poor unfortunate was cooped up in the house behind us, not able to get out; and I beheld with fascinated eye straggling twos and threes of women stealing through the orchard in search of the W.C. and slinking hurriedly back when they beheld the Earl and me gallantly holding the fort!"[3]

Attractions and Activities

Bright River Station

The Bright River Station and Tea Room is on the north side of Route 2 in Hunter River, on the site of the old train station. Island crafts are for sale at the site. Sadly, the train station has been removed. In fact, the historic role of the railway on PEI is finished forever — not one train runs here any more.

Bright River, the train station in *Anne of Green Gables*, was modelled on the Hunter River Station.[4] It was here that MATTHEW (and millions of enchanted readers) first met ANNE. "The long platform was almost deserted; the only living creature in sight being a girl who was sitting on a pile of shingles at the extreme end. Matthew, barely noting that it *was* a girl, sidled past her as quickly as possible without looking at her. Had he looked he could hardly have failed to notice the tense rigidity and expectation of

Another form of transportation in Lucy Maud Montgomery's day — cutter sleigh, circa 1900

her attitude and expression. She was sitting there waiting for something or somebody and, since sitting and waiting was the only thing to do just then, she sat and waited with all her might and main."[5]

Notes:

1 Journals, Vol. 2, p. 10
2 Journals, Vol. 2, p. 11
3 Journals, Vol. 2, p. 15
4 Journals, vol. 2, p. 40
5 Anne of Green Gables, p. 13

KENSINGTON

"Finally we reached Kensington where we were informed that a special containing Sir John and Lady Macdonald — who are touring the Island — would be along in an hour; so Grandpa...telegraphed to Hunter River for Sir John to stop at Kensington and take us on. I assure you I was quite excited over the prospect of seeing the Premier of Canada. When the special came I followed grandpa on board and the next moment was in the presence of the great man himself. He was very genial and motioned me to a seat between himself and Lady M. where I sat demurely and scrutinized them both out of the tail of my eye."

Journals, Volume 1, page 25

The Setting

Kensington is a major cross-roads for people travelling on PEI. It is located on the east side of Malpeque Bay.

If you are you are coming from downtown Charlottetown, first find University Avenue and head north out of town. Bear west (right) where the road divides just past the Peter Pan Drive-In, and take Route 2 through Hunter River to Kensington (48 kilometres).

If you are arriving on the Island by the Borden ferry, just follow the traffic out of the village. After about 8 kilometres you'll come to an underpass where the road divides. Follow the signs for Summerside and head north on Route 1A for 20 kilometres. Turn east (right) at Traveller's Rest and continue on the Blue Heron Drive (Route 2) for 8 kilometres to Kensington.

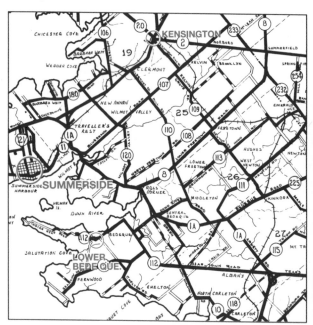

As you drive from Traveller's Rest to Kensington you will see prime Island farm land all around you. Seed potatos are an important crop here, as they are throughout the Island. Here and there strips of green woodland mark the boundaries of fields. If you look to the left you may see the Indian River Church glinting white in the distance. In the town of Kensington old historic buildings rest alongside the new. People here are busy — there is much to be done before the harvest season, and in the summer a lot of people pass through.

In the early days of the community there were only four houses, and the village was known as Five Lanes End. The name referred to the roads from Charlottetown, Mill Valley, Summerside, Malpeque and Margate. In 1824 Five Lanes End was named

Kensington Train Station, circa 1905

Barrett's Cross after Tom and Maggie Barrett, who operated Barrett's Inn and were active members of the community. In 1862 Kensington was formed from the old communities of Barrett's Cross and Margate. Old-timers may still refer to it as Barrett's Cross.[1]

The community grew as a result of its location: people travelling by train or buggy stopped in Kensington long enough to spend their money in the local businesses. And although the railway no longer runs on Prince Edward Island, many people still pass through the town by car. Kensington is in the centre of a large farming community, of which dairy and potato farms are the most common. Many people are also employed at the local potato processing plant — Cavendish Farms.

Tourism is important in the area. The town welcomes travellers to museums, craft shops, good places to eat and a variety of other services. The roads out of town lead to some of the best-loved tourist spots on the Island.

About L.M. Montgomery

When Maud was young, the railway was still the major form of long-distance travel. It was at the old Kensington Station that 15-year-old Maud met Sir John A. and Lady Macdonald. (See the quotation at the beginning of the chapter.)

But even during Maud's lifetime one sure sign of change could be seen — automobiles. It took a while for the automobile to become popular on the Island, and early laws confined its use to specific areas and certain days of the week. There were even reports of determined car owners loading their cars on the train in order to reach a place where road travel was permitted. By Maud's adulthood, however, she noted with mixed sentiments that the automobile was here to stay: "In one way I'm rather pleased. I hate to hear the Island made fun of for its prejudice against cars. On the other hand I resent their presence in this haunt of ancient peace. I wanted it kept sacred to the gods of the old time. I wanted to think that there was one place in the world where the strident honk-honk of a car-horn could never jar on the scented air."[2]

When Maud travelled by horse and buggy, she was able to absorb the natural beauty of the Island countryside. She savoured the moment and brought each roadside scene to life in words. "We drove home from Kensington through the cold, frosty moonlit night. As we drove up a long Irishtown hill I was suddenly impressed with the weird, striking beauty of the moonlight falling through the spruce trees along the road — alternate bars of shadow and silver. It was a road peculiar to P.E. Island."[3]

Attractions and Activities

Kensington Visitor Information Centre

The Visitor Information Centre, which is operated by the Kensington and Area Tourism Association, is housed in the 1904 Train Station Building. It is on Route 20, about one block north of the main intersection in Kensington (where Routes 2, 6, 20 and 101 meet), on the west side of the road. The friendly staff will help you with your travel on the Island, whether you are planning as you go and want to know where vacancies can be found, looking for a beach full of people, or seeking out a quiet nook. Local handicrafts and other products are also available here.

Perhaps, like ANNE, you just want to enjoy a quiet drive down scenic back roads. When ANNE first arrived on the Island, she loved to drive on the red clay roads, feasting her eyes on the beautiful scenery. "This Island is the bloomiest place. I just love it already, and I'm so glad I'm going to live here. I've always heard that Prince Edward Island was the prettiest place in the world, and I used to imagine I was living here, but I never really expected I would. It's delightful when your imaginations come true, isn't it? But those red roads are so funny."[4]

St. Mary's Roman Catholic Church

Drive north out of Kensington on Route 20 for about 5 kilometres to the intersection of Route 104. Turn west (left) here and drive a few kilometres to Indian River. You can't miss the white spires of St. Mary's, an impressive church in the French-gothic style, designed by noted Island architect W.C. Harris.

Throughout the summer, a series of Sunday concerts is usually offered at this church. Concerts are an old Island tradition, a way to bring the com-

St. Mary's Roman Catholic Church

munity together, and were a preferred form of entertainment for ANNE and her friends. In summer they would travel by buggy to the nearby villages, and in the winter they would go by sleigh. "They all crowded into the big pung sleigh, among straw and furry robes. Anne reveled in the drive to the hall, slipping along over the satin-smooth roads with the snow crisping under the runners. There was a magnificent sunset, and the snowy hills and deep blue water of the St. Lawrence Gulf seemed to rim in the splendor like a huge bowl of pearl and sapphire brimmed with wine and fire. Tinkles of sleigh-bells and distant laughter, that seemed like the mirth of wood elves, came from every quarter."[5]

Notes:
1   The History of Kensington, pp. 6, 83
2   Journals, Vol. 2, p. 250
3   Journals, Vol. 2, p. 275
4   Anne of Green Gables, p. 14
5   Anne of Green Gables, p. 152

LOWER BEDEQUE

"As for my school, I am not overburdened with work as there are only fourteen *children in the district. Imagine the contrast to the large schools I have had! But a couple of advanced students give me comfortably enough to do and I simply* love *teaching here....I feel as if I have lived in Bedeque all my life."*

Journals, Volume 1, page 203

The Setting

Look on your map and you will see Lower Bedeque in the area south of Kensington and Summerside.

From Kensington, drive 8 kilometres west toward Summerside on Route 2. When you reach Travellers Rest, turn south (left) onto Route 1A and follow it for 10 kilometres to Central Bedeque. Turn west (right) at Central Bedeque and follow Route 10 for 2 kilometres. Take another right (north) turn onto Route 112 and follow as it curves into Lower Bedeque (about 3 kilometres).

If you are travelling from Charlottetown, go west on the Trans-Canada Highway (Routes 1 and 1A) for 57 kilometres until you come to Central Bedeque. Turn west (left) here and follow Route 10 for two kilometres. Then turn north (right) onto Route 112 and follow it for 3 kilometres into Lower Bedeque.

Lower Bedeque is a peninsula jutting out into the Summerside Harbour, bordered by the beautiful Dunk River to the north and the warm waters of Northumberland Strait to the south.

As you drive along the winding road through Lower Bedeque you will see well-kept farms with level land running down to the water's edge. Note the

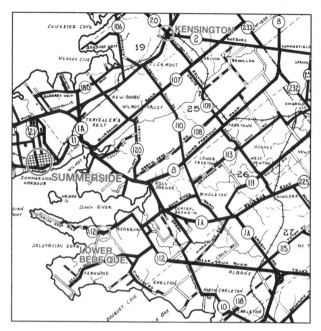

clear view of the water on both sides of the peninsula. Follow the road to the end, and you will see the town of Summerside across the bay. Note also the pleasant beach, dotted with several cottages. The water here is about the warmest you will find on Prince Edward Island, and the swimming is great.

The economy of Lower Bedeque is based on dairy, potato and hog farming. Most farms here are not mixed — rather, Lower Bedeque is a community of different kinds of specialized farms.

Bedeque is the spelling used by early French settlers for the Micmac word "eptek", meaning "hot" or "ebedek", meaning "hot place". Each winter, because the south side of the Island is much warmer than the north side, Malpeque area Micmacs moved from the North Shore to Bedeque.

A croquet game in Lower Bedeque, circa 1911

About L.M. Montgomery

Maud's third and last teaching post, for the 1897-1898 term, was in Lower Bedeque. She came here after a year of study at Dalhousie University in Halifax, and she enjoyed herself: "The people are so nice, friendly, and sociable. It is a lively place with lots of young people and I have had a lively time."[1]

It was while boarding with Mr. and Mrs. Cornelius Leard in Lower Bedeque that Maud met her first real love — she fell passionately in love with the Leard's son, Herman. But she believed that she could not find lasting happiness with Herman because he was not her equal. "I would not have *married* him for anything. He was my inferior in every respect. This is not vanity on my part at all. He simply was. He had no brains, no particular good looks, in short, nothing that I admire in a man. Yet I loved him as I never can love any other man."[2]

Maud's time in Lower Bedeque ended suddenly in March of 1898. Her grandfather Alexander Macneill

Lower Bedeque School

died, and Maud returned to Cavendish to care for her aging grandmother, Lucy Woolner Macneill.

In July of 1899, just one year after Maud left Lower Bedeque, Herman Leard died after several weeks of illness believed to have been caused by influenza. Some say he died of a broken heart.

Attractions and Activities

Lower Bedeque School

To find the Lower Bedeque school where Maud taught, follow Route 112 west onto the Lower Bedeque peninsula. The school is located on the south (left) side of the road. It has been restored and is typical of the one-room schoolhouses that were once common on the Island.

Maud's happiness at the Lower Bedeque school may have inspired her description of ANNE'S joy on her first day of school in Avonlea: " 'What a splendid day!' said Anne, drawing a long breath. 'Isn't it good

Lower Bedeque School, interior

just to be alive on a day like this? I pity the people who aren't born yet for missing it.' "[3]

At the Lower Bedeque school you can look around at the old furnishings, books and written materials. Students who work at the site for the summer will be happy to tell you the history of the school building and explain how it was restored.

Holman Island

From Lower Bedeque it is a twenty minute walk across the sand — at low tide — to Holman Island in Summerside Harbour. In about half an hour you can walk around the little Island, and another twenty minutes will have you back in Lower Bedeque in lots of time before high tide. At low tide you can also walk to the lighthouse in the harbour.

Notes:

1   Journals, Vol. 1, p. 203
2   My Dear Mr. M., p. 29
3   Anne of Green Gables, p. 105

MALPEQUE

"Hugh Montgomery came to Canada from Scotland. He sailed on a vessel bound for Quebec; but the fates and a woman's will took a hand in the thing. His wife was desperately seasick all the way across the Atlantic — and a voyage over the Atlantic was no five days' run then. Off the north shore of Prince Edward Island, then a wild, wooded land, with settlements few and far between, the Captain hove-to in order to replenish his supply of water. He sent a boat ashore, and he told poor Mrs. Montgomery that she might go in it for a little change. Mrs. Montgomery did go in it; and when she felt that blessed dry land under her feet once more, she told her husband that she meant to stay there. Never again would she set foot in any vessel....So the Montgomerys came to Prince Edward Island."

The Alpine Path, page 12

The Setting

You will find Malpeque in the central region of the Island, on the northeast side of Malpeque Bay. It is about 32 kilometres west of Cavendish on the Blue Heron Scenic Drive. Take Route 6 southwest from Cavendish all the way to New London and then turn north (right) onto Route 20. Follow Route 20 north and west from New London along the North Shore right into Malpeque. You can also find Malpeque by driving about 11 kilometres northwest from Kensington, on Route 20 (also part of the Blue Heron Scenic Drive).

Malpeque is an Island haven where rich red soil from fertile farmland slopes down to the wide Mal-

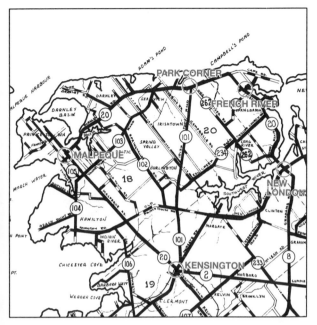

peque Bay. The Bay empties into the Gulf of St. Lawrence, but a stretch of sandbar protects it from the full force of the Gulf shore winds. This is a perfect place for canoeing, wind-surfing and peaceful walks along the shore. If you like to explore, take a drive down any side road and you may discover your very own stretch of sandy beach.

Malpeque Harbour is a lively setting, typical of most Island fishing ports. You will see Island fishers putting their wooden boats out to sea, unloading their catches, or patiently mending their equipment. If you are hoping for a deep-sea fishing adventure, this is an ideal spot to find an experienced skipper.

There is also stocked trout fishing nearby, for those who like to fish but want to stay close to dry land. Even ANNE and DIANA enjoyed an afternoon of

trout fishing. "It was splendid to fish for trout over
the bridge and the two girls learned to row themselves about in the little flat-bottomed dory Mr.
Barry kept for duck shooting."[1]

Malpeque is a French version of the Micmac word
"makpaak", meaning "large bay". Fishing and farming are the area's main industries, and the famous
Malpeque oysters have brought considerable fortune
to the region.

About L.M. Montgomery

Hugh and Mary McShannon Montgomery were
the great-great-grandparents of Lucy Maud Montgomery. In 1769, Mary McShannon Montgomery
chose the Island, that later nurtured Maud Montgomery, as her home. According to family legend,
they were also the first English-speaking settlers in
Malpeque, which was called Princetown at that time.

In Maud's time, Malpeque was the home of her
Aunt Emily and Uncle John. It was during a long
childhood visit here that she became chums with an
orphan girl, Maggie Abbott. The two girls swore eter-
nal friendship, just as ANNE and DIANA did in *Anne of
Green Gables*. "Only we did not do it in a garden,"
wrote Maud, "but standing on a high beam in Uncle
John Montgomery's barn at Malpeque."[2]

In her girlhood days, Maud travelled to Malpeque
from her home in Cavendish and from her Aunt
Annie Campbell's home at Silver Bush in Park Corner. As an adult, she came from her teaching posts at
Bideford and Belmont (on the other side of the bay),
and from Lower Bedeque (southeast of Malpeque).
Travel was by horse and buggy, or by cutter sleigh in
winter, and as Maud wrote "you may be sure our
drive was a merry one."[3]

There are some family members who still live in
the Malpeque area and the church cemetery in the

village testifies to the generations of Montgomerys who lived in this corner of the Island.

Attractions and Activities

Cabot Provincial Park

Drive north about 2 kilometres from Malpeque Corner and follow the signs to the park. (This road does not have a Route number because it is only open in the summer.) Cabot Provincial Park offers a Class A beach, supervised swimming, camping, golf, and a complete range of summer recreation activities. A park naturalist will be pleased to introduce you to bird watching and beach combing, and guide you along a series of hiking trails.

If you share the independent spirit of ANNE, you may prefer to explore the park on your own. ANNE was thrilled by the magical nature of Island woodlands, and spent many hours dreaming there. "That bridge led Anne's dancing feet up over a wooded hill beyond, where perpetual twilight reigned under the straight, thick-growing firs and spruces; the only flowers there were myriads of delicate 'June bells', those shyest and sweetest of woodland blooms ..."[4] You too can explore to your heart's content, delight in the salty ocean breezes, and enjoy the spectacular scenery from the many secluded beaches around Malpeque Bay.

The Keir Memorial Museum

The museum is housed in the former Keir Memorial Presbyterian Church on Route 20 in Malpeque. The collection has furnishings and handcrafts from long-established homesteads in Malpeque, including items from the home of Maud's Aunt Emily and Uncle John.

Malpeque Gardens

Malpeque Gardens

You will find this attraction, which prides itself on being "The Island's Show Garden," in the village of Malpeque on Route 20. The gardens feature special exhibits, including the Anne of Green Gables Gardens and a children's mini-farm. Some of Maud Montgomery's favourite flowers are in this exhibit, plus over 400 varieties of dahlia. On display are floral designs of MARILLA'S quilt, ANNE'S flowered hat, and a bottle of MARILLA'S currant wine.

ANNE'S flowered hat played a role in ANNE'S first day of Sunday school, when she wanted so much to fit in with the other girls. "Her hat was a little, flat, glossy, new sailor, the extreme plainness of which had likewise much disappointed Anne, who had permitted herself secret visions of ribbon and flowers. The latter, however, were supplied before Anne reached the main road, for being confronted half-way down the lane with a golden frenzy of wind-stirred buttercups and a glory of wild roses, Anne promptly and liberally garlanded her hat with a heavy wreath of them. Whatever other people might have thought of the result it satisfied Anne, and she tripped gaily down the road, holding her ruddy head with its decoration of pink and yellow very proudly."[5]

MARILLA'S currant wine played an important role in one of the more memorable scenes from *Anne of Green Gables*, the afternoon when ANNE invited DIANA BARRY over for tea. ANNE was delighted with her new friend, and she graciously served her guest MARILLA'S famous raspberry cordial. "I love bright red drinks, don't you? They taste twice as good as any other colour."[6] ANNE didn't realize, however, that she had taken the wrong bottle off the shelf and served DIANA some of MARILLA'S homemade red currant wine by mistake!

At the Malpeque Gardens gift shop, you may be lucky enough to find some local traditional-style knitting, much admired by Maud. She wrote that whenever she knitted a quilt, she thought of Malpeque.[7]

Notes:

1   Anne of Green Gables, p. 221
2   Journals, Vol 2, p. 42
3   Journals, Vol 1, p. 122
4   Anne of Green Gables p. 63
5   Anne of Green Gables, p. 80
6   Anne of Green Gables, p. 123
7   Journals, Vol. 2, p. 143

NEW LONDON

"Beyond Stanley the road wound on to another little village — Clifton. And here, around a certain corner, is a certain small, yellowish-brown house, close to the road, that I always look at with a kind of fascination, for it is the house where my father and mother lived after their marriage, and where I was born and spent the first year of my life. The years have passed on and each succeeding one has left the little brown house something shabbier than before, but its enchantment has never faded in my eyes. I always look for it with the same eager interest when I turn the corner...."

Journals, Volume 1, page 230

The Setting

You will find New London by travelling 11 kilometres west from Cavendish. Take route 6 on the Blue Heron Drive. You'll cross both the Hope River (at Bayview) and the Stanley River (at Stanley Bridge) before arriving in lovely New London, on the bank of the Southwest River. If you are coming from Kensington, take Route 6 northeast for 11 kilometres through Margate and Clinton to New London.

Against a backdrop of gentle, rolling hills this peaceful village overlooks the glinting blue expanse of New London Harbour. The Southwest River flows calmly by the wharf, where deep-sea fishing boats put in for the night. You can take a boat ride from the wharf here and witness the breathtaking beauty of a summer sunset on New London Harbour.

If you are an early riser you'll see the the lobster boats putting out from the wharf for the day's catch.

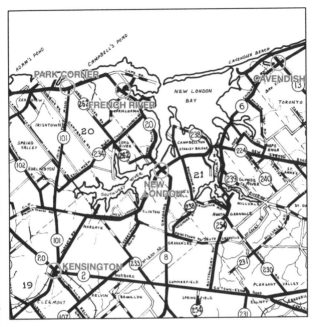

New London Harbour and the Gulf of St. Lawrence provide fishers in the area with lobster, quahaugs, oysters and mussels. Further inland, farmers seed the land to grow those famous Island potatoes. The handiwork of Island craftspeople is marketed in the many small communities of the area.

Just a few kilometres east on Route 6 is Stanley Bridge, one of the prettiest villages on the Island. It's surrounded by water on three sides and across the harbour you can see the white dunes of the sandspit shimmering in the sunlight. A picnic featuring fresh lobster is a treat not to be missed while you visit this area.

The name New London was first given to a small settlement on the west side of New London Bay near the French River Inlet. It was named by Robert

New London lobster boats

Clark, a Quaker merchant from London, England who owned the land in the area. In 1773 he arrived in the bay, bringing with him a company of about 100 people. They formed the first New London settlement.[1]

In Maud's lifetime New London referred to the area around the present day communities of French River and Springbrook.[2] By 1880 the district of New London Post Office had been moved across the Southwest River to Clifton — as a result, the village formerly called Clifton is now known as New London.

About L.M. Montgomery

"I was born in the little village of Clifton, Prince Edward Island. 'Old Prince Edward Island' is a good place in which to be born — a good place in which to spend a childhood. I can think of none better."[3]

Lucy Maud Montgomery was born the daughter of Clara Woolner Macneill and Hugh John Montgomery on November 30, 1874. Her father operated Clifton House, the village general store. Shortly after giving birth, Clara became ill with tuberculosis, and died at her parents' home in Cavendish when her daughter was only 21 months old. After his wife's death Hugh John left the store and headed out west to Prince Albert, Saskatchewan. Lucy Maud stayed on with her maternal grandparents, the Macneills, in Cavendish.

Clifton House burned down a few years later, but Lucy Maud Montgomery's birthplace is still standing. In 1964, the industrialist K.C. Irving deeded the home to the Province of Prince Edward Island. Restoration work followed. Since 1965 it has been run by the L.M. Montgomery Foundation Board, whose members are appointed by the Province.[4]

The village of Clifton (New London) was the half-way-point on Lucy Maud's trips from her home in Cavendish to her second home at Uncle John Campbell's farm in Park Corner.

Sometimes she attended church in Clifton. On one such occasion, when Lucy Maud was about four years old, she and her Aunt Emily were at a service in the old Clifton Presbyterian Church. She was curious to know where Heaven was and asked her aunt about it. Not wanting to disrupt the service, her Aunt Emily didn't say anything; she just pointed upward. Lucy Maud was delighted to find out that her mother was up in the church attic! But why couldn't she visit her there? She swore when she grew up she would somehow get from Cavendish to Clifton and see her mother. As she later wrote in her journal, "When I was a child heaven was only seven miles away. But now! Is it not beyond the furthest star?"[5]

Nearby Stanley Bridge is a busy fishing village found on the Stanley River where it empties into New London Bay. For young Lucy Maud, this small community loomed large. "Stanley used to seem quite a town to my childish eyes. It was the hub of

The Lucy Maud Montgomery Birthplace

the universe then — or of our solar system at the very least."[6]

Attractions and Activities

Lucy Maud Montgomery Birthplace

You'll find this restored home from the 1850s in New London, on the north side of Route 6 just east of the corner where Routes 6 and 8 meet. The Birthplace museum is open daily from June through Thanksgiving. Visitors can see the room where Lucy Maud Montgomery was born, and absorb the atmosphere of the home and community that welcomed her into the world.

Lucy Maud Montgomery's wedding dress is on display here — it is made of cream crepe de Chine with ornamental lace and beadwork. ANNE dreamed of having such a dress, but without much hope. " 'I don't ever expect to be a bride myself. I'm so homely nobody will ever want to marry me — unless it might be a foreign missionary. I suppose a foreign mission-

Lucy Maud Montgomery's wedding dress

Scrapbooks in the Lucy Maud Montgomery Birthplace

ary mightn't be very particular. But I do hope that some day I shall have a white dress. That is my highest ideal of earthly bliss...' "[7]

Several of Lucy Maud Montgomery's personal scrapbooks are on display. In them she kept cut-out copies of her published stories and poems. She even saved some fur from her favourite cat, Daff.

Lucy Maud Montgomery's birthplace at Clifton was the model for the house where ANNE was born.[8] In *Anne of the Island*, ANNE returns to her first home and finds it almost exactly as she pictured it. " 'There is no honeysuckle over the windows, but there *is* a lilac tree by the gate, and — yes, there are the muslin curtains in the windows. How glad I am ... ' "[9]

PEI Marine Aquarium, Stanley Bridge

The Aquarium is in Stanley Bridge on Route 6, 5 kilometres east of New London. Here you can see fish and seals native to Maritime waters. Other exhibits feature birds, butterflies, oysters and shells.

Notes:
1   The Parish of New London, p. 2
2   French River and Park Corner History, p. 11
3   The Alpine Path, p. 10
4   Kindred Spirits of P.E.I., Spring 1990, p. 6
5   Journals, Vol. 2, p. 45
6   Journals, Vol. 1, p. 230
7   Anne of Green Gables, p. 13
8   Journals, Vol. 2, p. 41
9   Anne of the Island, p. 146

PARK CORNER

"...This is certainly the greatest house in the world for fun. We have had so many jolly rackets here that the very walls seem to be permeated with the essence of 'good times'. From my earliest recollection a visit to Park Corner was the greatest treat in the world. Each room has its memories - the kitchen where we toasted our toes at the glowing old 'Waterloo', the front rooms where we spent so many jolly evenings, the big bedrooms upstairs where we slept and talked; and best of all, that famous old pantry, stored with good things, into which it was our habit to crowd at bedtime and gnaw bones, crunch fruitcake and scream with laughter. That pantry is historical."

Journals, Volume 1, page 257

The Setting

Park Corner is on the north shore, about 20 kilometres from Cavendish.

If you are travelling from Cavendish, drive southwest on Route 6 and follow the beautiful Blue Heron Drive through Bayview and Stanley Bridge to New London (11 kilometres). At New London you turn northwest (right) onto Route 20 and cross the Southwest river, following the Blue Heron Drive for 10 kilometres to Park Corner.

You can also find Park Corner by taking Route 101 north for 12 kilometres from Kensington. You will pass through Burlington and Irishtown before you come to Park Corner.

If you feel like getting away from it all, Park Corner is a good place to relax. Several roads branch off

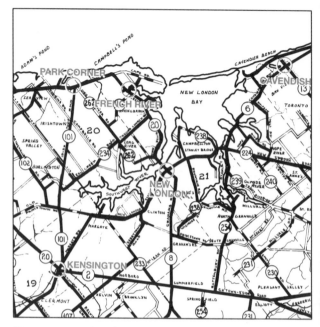

Route 20 to the shore. A five minute drive will take you to a lovely beach with no crowds.

Park Corner is composed of a wonderful patchwork of green fields, sand dunes and ponds strung along the shoreline. It is a clean community with well-kept homesteads. The economy is farm-based — there are some mixed farms in the area, but most are dairy farms.

Maud is the great-great granddaughter of James Townsend, the Englishman who named Park Corner after his old home in England. Townsend was given land in the area in return for his military services. He and his family settled here in 1775.

Silver Bush, at Park Corner

About L.M. Montgomery

To Maud, visiting Park Corner was sheer joy. Here she spent many happy hours with her aunt Annie (Macneill) Campbell, uncle John Campbell and the cousins who were her childhood companions. "Uncle John Campbell's house was a big white one, smothered in orchards. Here, in other days, there was a trio of merry cousins to rush out and drag me in with greeting and laughter. The very walls of that house must have been permeated by the essence of good times."[1]

The Campbell house was Maud's second home. It provided her with some of the beautiful surroundings she was later to describe in her books. The magnificent maple and beech grove behind the Campbell house inspired the Silver Bush setting for Maud's books *Pat of Silverbush* and *Mistress Pat*. During visits to the Island after her marriage, Maud and her two sons spent much of their time at the Campbell home in Park Corner.

Ruth and George Campbell

The Campbell home has been handed down from father to son since the eighteenth century, when the first Campbells settled in the old homestead. It was built in 1872 by John Campbell, who married Maud's favourite aunt, Annie Macneill of Cavendish. Now known as Silver Bush, it is the presently the home of Ruth Campbell, who was raised in Malpeque by Maud's cousin, James Montgomery. Ruth also has connections with the maternal side of Maud's family — she married the grandson of Annie Macneill Campbell. Part of the house is reserved for the Anne of Green Gables Museum, which is operated by Ruth and her son George. George Campbell also publishes a newsletter called *Kindred Spirits of P.E.I.*, which pays tribute to the works of L.M. Montgomery and describes the period of Island history in which she lived.

The old house across the road from the museum was the home of another famous relative of Maud, her grandfather Senator Donald Montgomery. It is not open for tours.

The Green Gables Museum at Silver Bush

Attractions and Activities

Anne of Green Gables Museum at Silver Bush

You will find the Anne of Green Gables Museum on Route 20 in Park Corner. If you have come from Kensington on Route 101 you turn right onto Route 20. The museum is on the south (right) side of the road. If you are driving west from Cavendish, it will be on your left.

The Anne of Green Gables Museum is housed in the two-storey Campbell home. Now called Silver Bush, it is painted white, with green trim, and is surrounded by orchards, shrubs and flowers. The museum displays a large collection of artifacts about Lucy Maud Montgomery and *Anne of Green Gables*, and offers a guided tour through the large, airy rooms.

It was here that Maud married Reverend Ewan Macdonald in 1911; each year on July 5, their wedding is re-enacted on the site.

Green Gables Museum, interior

In the museum, you can see the organ on which Maud's wedding march was played, the room Maud used when she stayed here, and the bookcase she described in *Anne of Green Gables*: "We used to pretend that the bookcase was enchanted and that if I only knew the spell I could open the door and step right into the room where Katie Maurice lived, instead of into Mrs. Thomas' shelves of preserves and china. And then Katie Maurice would have taken me by the hand and led me out into a wonderful place, all flowers and sunshine and fairies, and we would have lived there happy for ever after."[2]

Other items of interest at the museum are autographed first editions of Maud's books; her letters; and her grandfather Macneill's armchair. You can even see the knob on the stair wall where young Maud measured her height.

The Lake of Shining Waters

Lake of Shining Waters

The Lake of Shining Waters is at Silver Bush and is commonly known as Campbell's Pond. You can find it just east of the Campbell homestead.

Maud's bedroom window at the Campbell home gave her a splendid view of the Pond, which she named the Lake of Shining Waters, and later wrote about in her novels. In *Anne of Green Gables*, ANNE is overcome with the beauty of the lake when she sees it for the first time. " 'I shall call it — let me see — the Lake of Shining Waters. Yes, that is the right name for it. I know because of the thrill. When I hit on a name that suits exactly it gives me a thrill.' "[3]

One of the best-loved scenes in *Anne of Green Gables,* when ANNE first tastes ice-cream, is also set beside Maud's favourite lake. " 'Oh, Marilla,' she exclaimed breathlessly, 'there's going to be a Sunday school picnic next week — in Mr. Harmon Andrews' field, right near the Lake of Shining Waters. And Mrs. Superintendent Bell and Mrs. Rachel Lynde are going to make ice-cream — think of it, Marilla — *ice-cream!* And oh, Marilla, can I go to it?' "[4]

Surrounding the lake, green farm fields slope close to the water's edge. There is a marshy area as well, and at one end the lake is sheltered from the Gulf of St. Lawrence by big sand hills.

You are welcome to take a walk by the lake, or fish, or go for a paddle if you have a canoe. Or, like ANNE, you can simply relax with a picnic and appreciate its beauty.

Notes:
1 The Alpine Path, p. 43
2 Anne of Green Gables, p. 58
3 Anne of Green Gables, p. 19
4 Anne of Green Gables, p. 90

ANNE DAY TOUR

This day tour is for the most energetic of ANNE and Lucy Maud Montgomery fans. It begins bright and early and winds up at 10 pm. If you prefer a shorter day, simply head for home whenever the spirit moves you. When you get hungry, stop for a picnic and enjoy the breath-taking scenery, or visit one of the many good restaurants along the way.

Plan to begin your ANNE tour in Cavendish at 9 am. If you must first travel to Cavendish, give your-self enough time to get there — if you are coming by car from Charlottetown, you should allow yourself forty-five minutes. Once in Cavendish, we suggest that you park your car near one of the many ANNE attractions and walk to the others, following the signs. For those who prefer driving, it is also possible to drive from place to place. Either way, it will take about two hours to see the spots loved by Maud and filled with the spirit of ANNE.

The tour starts at The Site of L.M. Montgomery's Cavendish Home, on Route 6, just east of Route 13. You will see the sign for it almost immediately on the south side of the road, just past the Cavendish United Church. The Cavendish Home is where Maud lived and found the inspiration to write *Anne of Green Gables*. Her Macneill relatives have restored the grounds and site of the old Macneill farmhouse and have preserved the original apple trees under which Maud sat as a girl and young woman.

Next, be sure to take a tour of Green Gables House, in Prince Edward Island National Park. Green Gables House is off Route 6, just west of the intersection of Routes 6 and 13. This was once the farmhouse of Margaret and David Macneill, cousins of Maud's grandfather. Maud often visited their farm and she used it as the principal setting for *Anne of*

Green Gables. Carefully restored and furnished as described in the book, Green Gables House will transport you into the life and time of ANNE.

From Green Gables House, you can take a short stroll down Lover's Lane and follow the Babbling Brook along the Balsam Hollow Trail. The Haunted Wood Trail, also within walking distance, leads through a dark spruce grove to the site of Maud's old schoolhouse and then into the Cavendish cemetery. Interpretive signs are placed along both trails to highlight their significance for L.M. Montgomery and ANNE.

Explore the Cavendish cemetery, as Maud was fond of doing, at the southwest corner of Routes 6 and 13. Maud and her husband Ewan Macdonald are buried here, as well as Maud's mother, Clara Macneill Montgomery, and her grandparents.

Just past the southeast corner of the intersection of Routes 6 and 13 in Cavendish are the Green Gables Post Office and, beside it, the Cavendish United Church. The church was Presbyterian in Maud's day and is now the scene for the annual L.M. Montgomery inter-faith memorial service in August. Don't miss the exhibit at the Green Gables Post Office, explaining the important role that mail played in Maud's life here.

At 11 am, you should be driving west on Route 6 from Cavendish to New London. You will pass through scenic Stanley Bridge just before arriving. In New London, be sure to visit the Lucy Maud Montgomery Birthplace, at the intersection of Routes 6 and 20. Plan to spend 30 minutes here, to get the feel of the home and countryside where Maud was born. Inside the house, several of her personal scrapbooks and her wedding dress are on display.

From New London, take Route 20 northwest, through French River to Park Corner. If you have some time, take a four kilometre detour at French River and visit the Cape Tryon Lighthouse. If you are hungry, the breath-taking north shore is a perfect picnic-stop, or visit one of our famous restaurants — you are sure to find fresh lobster throughout the summer.

You should arrive in Park Corner around 2:30 pm. Stay for an hour to enjoy the Anne of Green Gables Museum and the Lake of Shining Waters — all part of Silver Bush, the Campbell farm. The Campbells, who are relatives of Maud, still own and operate the museum. They also publish a newsletter called *Kindred Spirits of P.E.I.*, which celebrates the life and times of L.M. Montgomery.

From Park Corner, follow Route 20 further west to Malpeque. Colourful Malpeque Gardens is a relaxing site for an afternoon walk, and displays some of Maud's favourite flowers. When you are ready, follow Route 20 south to Kensington. If you like, take a short detour onto Route 104, into Indian River. Here you can see the impressive St. Mary's Roman Catholic Church, designed in the French-gothic style by famous Island architect W.C. Harris.

When you get to Kensington, visit the old train station that was so important to travellers in Maud's time. Then take Route 2 east to Hunter River and on to Charlottetown.

Your final stop is Charlottetown, where you can cap off your day with a performance of *Anne of Green Gables* in the Confederation Centre. (Make sure you have booked your tickets in advance.) Plan to be at the theatre by 7:45 pm. The performance begins at 8 pm and ends at about 10 pm.

Your day is now complete — in the course of your travels, you will have visited most of the places that inspired Maud to create ANNE, and compelled her to write with such passion about this Island home.

Select Bibliography

The Alpine Path: the Story of My Career. L.M. Montgomery. Fitzhenry & Whiteside, Toronto, Ontario, 1975 (First published in 1917).

Anne of Avonlea. L.M. Montgomery. Seal, Toronto, 1981 (First published in 1909).

Anne of Green Gables. L.M. Montgomery. Seal, Toronto, 1981 (First published in 1908).

Anne of The Island. L.M. Montgomery. Seal, Toronto, 1981 (First published in 1915).

Anne's House of Dreams. L.M. Montgomery. Seal, Toronto, 1981 and McClelland & Stewart, Toronto, 1989 (First published in 1917).

French River and Park Corner History 1773 - 1973. Eldon and Evelyn Foster. Coronation Women's Institute, Prince Edward Island, 1973.

The Green Gables Letters, From L.M. Montgomery to Ephraim Weber 1905 - 1909. Wilfrid Eggleston, Editor. Borealis Press, Ottawa, 1981.

The History of Kensington. Kensington Lions Club, Kensington, PEI, 1973.

A History of the Parish of New London, Prince Edward Island. Thomas Reagh Millman. Toronto, Ontario, 1959.

Kindred Spirits of P.E.I.. Kindred Spirits of P.E.I., Golden Road, Prince Edward Island.

My Dear Mr. M: Letters to G.B. MacMillan from L.M. Montgomery. Francis W.P. Bolger and Elizabeth R. Epperly, Eds. McGraw-Hill Ryerson Limited, Toronto, 1980.

Prince Edward Island. L.M. Montgomery. In *The Spirit of Canada: Dominion and Provinces, 1939.* Canadian Pacific Railway, Montreal, 1939.

Selected Journals of L.M. Montgomery - Volume I: 1889 - 1910. Mary Rubio and Elizabeth Waterston, Eds. Oxford University Press Canada, Toronto, 1985

The Selected Journals of L.M. Montgomery - Volume II: 1910 - 1921. Mary Rubio and Elizabeth Waterson, Editors. Oxford University Press Canada, Toronto, 1987

Spirit Of Place, Lucy Maud Montgomery and Prince Edward Island. Francis W.P. Bolger, Ed. Oxford University Press Canada, Toronto, 1982.

The Wheel of Things: A Biography of L.M. Montgomery, Author of "Anne of Green Gables". Mollie Gillen. Fitzhenry & Whiteside, Toronto, 1975.

Index of Featured Attractions

L.M. Montgomery, 1908

"*Peace! You never know what peace is until you walk on the shores or in the fields or along the winding red roads of Abegweit on a summer twilight when the dew is falling and the old, old stars are peeping out and the sea keeps its nightly tryst with the little land it loves. You find your soul then. You realize that youth is not a vanished thing but something that dwells forever in the heart. And you look around on the dimming landscape of haunted hills and long white sand beaches and murmuring ocean, on homestead lights and the old fields tilled by the dead and gone generations who loved them...even if you are not Abegweit born, you will say, 'Why, I have come home.'*"

"Prince Edward Island" from *The Spirit Of Canada*